To Alice
with my best
wishes

Dr. John
11/15/09

Better Makes Us Best

Better Makes Us Best

▼

Dr. John Psarouthakis

Foreword by
Norman Bodek, President
Productivity, Inc.

Introduction by
Gilbert R. Whitaker, Jr., Dean
School of Business Administration,
University of Michigan

Productivity Press
Cambridge, Massachusetts and Norwalk, Connecticut

Productivity Press, Inc.
P.O. Box 3007
Cambridge, Massachusetts 02140
United States of America
Telephone: (617) 497-5146
Fax: (617) 868-3524

Library of Congress Catalog Card Number: 89-61158
ISBN: 0-915299-56-9

Cover design by Joyce C. Weston
Typeset by Rudra Press, Cambridge, MA
Printed and bound by Arcata/Halliday
Printed in the United States of America

Library of Congress Cataloging-in-Publication Data

Psarouthakis, John, 1932–
    Better makes us best.

    1. Labor productivity   2. Performance   3. Organizational effectiveness   I. Title
HD57.P76   1989   658.3'14   89-61158
ISBN 0-915299-56-9

89   90   91   10   9   8   7   6   5   4   3   2   1

Dedication

To my wife, Inga, for understanding the efforts and sacrifices needed in order to do better and for her spirited and inspiring support.

To my sons, Michael and Peter, who endured my long hours and my frequent and extended trips.

To my aunt Elisabeth Paleologou, who instilled in me early in life the importance of trying to do better.

To the employees of J.P. Industries, for taking to heart the philosophy and importance of doing better and for helping the corporation reach higher and higher levels of excellence.

To all, I'm deeply indebted.

J.P.

Table of Contents

Publisher's Foreword

"It's amazing what people can do with effort over time," says John Psarouthakis, founder and president of JP Industries. Dr. Psarouthakis — known as Dr. John to his employees — might have been thinking of how far he's come from his homeland, the Greek island of Crete. Orphaned at an early age, Psarouthakis was cared for by an aunt until he came to this country in 1952 to study engineering at MIT. At the time, he knew fewer than 100 words of English.

"Are you familiar," he continues, "with the great ancient Greek orator Demosthenes? Well, he was a stutterer, and the way he solved his problem was to go to the sea coast alone for years where he practiced speaking to the waves until he overcame his impediment. But it took time. He improved gradually. That was the key."

And that, in a nutshell, describes Psarouthakis's approach to continuous improvement. It's a philosophy he began developing from observations he made in the classrooms and on the playing fields of his youth: "I got equal satisfaction if I did better than last time, even though I also wanted to be best." The simplicity of this revelation is clearly presented in the delightful little book you now hold in your hands.

"Better is as better does," he writes in Chapter Four. "Each person, each day. Not startling productivity increases by super heroes." Underlying this philosophy of sensible, incremental improvement is a fundamental respect for the integrity and potential of each employee. Note, for example, how Psarouthakis answered when I asked him

what advice he would offer leaders seeking to promote a
better flow of communication from the plant floor through
various layers of management:

> I would say it's extremely important for a manager to
> understand that the structure which gives him or her
> authority is an artificial one. You must *never* forget
> that the people who work for you are unique indi-
> viduals who want to participate as much as possible
> in the improvement and success of the company.

Not surprisingly, Psarouthakis attributes JP Industries'
success to the *Better Makes Us Best* philosophy. Since 1979, the
company, which is headquartered in Ann Arbor, Michigan,
has continued to grow by acquiring and turning around
under-performing manufacturers of durable goods — from
plumbing supplies to engine parts to doorknobs and locks.

In its first year of operations, JP Industries employed 56
people. By 1988, that figure rose to its current level of 7,000
and revenues topped a half-billion dollars. Over the past
five years, sales have improved eightfold and net income has
grown at an annual rate of 35 percent.

As you've already gathered, there's nothing mysterious
about the *Better Makes Us Best* approach. It simply places a
premium on people. It encourages skill development, the
elimination of wasted effort and knowledge, and the creation of clear channels of communication. Of course, it also
insists on improvement and, even more importantly, teaches
a sensible approach to improvement through individual
goal-setting.

In these increasingly competitive times, we're seeing that
a company's success depends, more than ever, upon the kind
of team approach that Psarouthakis promotes. It's an approach that empowers every individual to take responsibility for a company's success by looking each day for ways to

improve his or her performance in small ways. Improvement doesn't just happen, though. A company's managers must see to it that employees are excited about participating in the improvement process.

It was with this goal in mind that Psarouthakis originally wrote and had *Better Makes Us Best* privately printed for his 7,000-member workforce. It reflects the spirit of a leader who's not only established a goal of being "the best," but one who knows precisely what this means. The concept of incremental improvement is a basic one, really. But as Psarouthakis points out, "In our modern societies, the sophisticated, the esoteric, and the convoluted often seem to be more in vogue than the simple, the basic, the straight-forward."

We think so, too. That's why we're proud to publish *Better Makes Us Best*. This little book is an important one. I know it's strengthened our resolve to be the best we can be. I think you'll be similarly inspired.

I'm grateful to many people for the care and effort that went into making *Better Makes Us Best*: Our hard working production team of David Lennon and Esmé McTighe; cover designer Joyce Weston; and Caroline Kutil, Michele Seery, Gayle Joyce and Susan Cobb of Rudra Press for maintaining the highest quality in typesetting and layout. I especially want to thank *Total Employee Involvement Newsletter* Editor Bill Dickinson. His guiding vision made publication of this book possible.

Norman Bodek
President
Barry Shulak
Project Editor

Preface

After coming to the United States in November 1951 from Greece, I discovered many new things. One of them was a language rich with images. Many expressions with which people in the United States grew up were new to me and packed with meaning. To some people, these often-heard phrases might be trite, but to me they said important things about the character and values of this society.

One such phrase was, "Some people look at a glass and say it's half empty; I look at the same glass and say it's half full." Those words speak volumes about a very basic difference in the way some people look at the world.

Throughout my career I have looked at the glass and have seen it half full. The remaining half always seemed to represent opportunity. When, from time to time, people tell me they aren't happy with their performance, that they're only operating at fifty percent of their abilities, I tell them that's not necessarily something to be discouraged about. After all, it's just that much more opportunity to perform better in the future.

The important thing is not to stop with recognizing that opportunities are available. The next step — doing something about it — is the one that makes all the difference.

I have seen under-performance not only with individuals but also with entire companies. A strength of J.P. Industries has been identifying companies that are performing below their potential, bringing those companies into our fold and helping them perform better.

When we have looked at a company before acquiring it,

we haven't focused on the negative, on the fact that it was performing poorly. We have focused on the positive — that the company had some positive elements and had some good things going for it. That meant that with some changes and assistance it would do better and could possibly reach its potential.

Just as an under-performing company is unrewarding to its owners and employees, people performing at only a fraction of their capability don't feel satisfied, productive, or successful in their work. But the moment that people recognize the source of their frustration, they have taken the first and most important step on the road to improvement. From that moment on, they can take positive actions that will lead them to their potential and help them enjoy their work experience and benefit more from it.

We've seen that philosophy become reality at J.P. Industries. We've seen it proven that if each member of our company tries to do his or her job better every day, we become better individually, better as a company, and better than the competition.

We have learned that by doing better today than we did yesterday we can be successful, fulfilled and satisfied with our performance. And by pledging to try to do things better and reach higher and higher levels of excellence, we, in the process, can achieve our best.

That is what our philosophy, *Better Makes Us Best*, is all about. And that is why this book is for the people of J.P. Industries — the men and women who have shown how this concept works in the real world. It is a concept that has guided the growth of our company and helped shape its future. Together the people of J.P. Industries have become the living examples of *Better Makes Us Best*.

Dr. John Psarouthakis
Ann Arbor, Michigan
May 1989

Introduction

I was flattered to be asked to prepare an introduction for this book, because I greatly admire John Psarouthakis and his many accomplishments as founder and leader of J.P. Industries. Having to write the introduction also gave me the opportunity — one I enjoyed tremendously, by the way — to re-read with care the wisdom set forth in this small book.

American business, as you know, has been criticized recently because of the success overseas competitors have had penetrating markets once dominated by U.S. companies. Our export markets have been relatively diminished, in part because of currency differences caused by government deficits, and also because American products are having a harder time competing with overseas products in terms of quality.

Only in the last ten to twenty years have international markets become important to domestic manufacturers. During this time the world has become one market driven by global competition. Global competition absolutely requires that our firms and their employees — from the CEO to the person who sweeps up — become aware of the need for continuous improvement of *every* job and process. *Better Makes Us Best* can help you cultivate such an awareness by imparting an understanding of the fundamental principles of continuous improvement.

The power of the book lies in its theme, which is relevant for anyone involved, in *any* way, in producing a product or providing a service. It suggests that to improve you must move forward with any given task at hand, do it well, look for the next possible improvement, do it well, and so on. Over time, as Psarouthakis has shown with J.P. Industries, the cumulative effect of such improvements can have a substantial positive effect.

Trying for the absolute best tomorrow is easy to imagine, but it's far too difficult a goal to achieve. On the other hand, trying your best to be better today, tomorrow, the day after tomorrow, and so on, is an achievable goal and will help you become *your* best. This message is so simply stated in the book that some readers may say it contains nothing new.

But deeper reflection will lead such readers to a much more valuable conclusion: However simple Psarouthakis's improvement message appears to be, making it happen in the workplace, both individually and collectively, is very challenging indeed. Getting started, in fact, may be the most difficult part. That's because it's all too easy to do today exactly what we did yesterday without giving any thought to how we might do it better.

In short, I highly recommend that anyone interested in improving the quality of products, services, and ultimately, the experience of work itself, read and consider the message in this book. I urge you to take note of the fact that this message has meaning for *every* employee, not just those on the shop floor.

Gilbert R. Whitaker, Jr., Dean
School of Business Administration
The University of Michigan

Better Makes Us Best

What Does
Better Makes Us Best
Really Mean?

It isn't really how much talent one has that matters. It's how much use we make of it that counts. We've all seen that proven time and again.

Dr. Norman Vincent Peale, author of *The Power of Positive Thinking*, once recalled a comment about his own personal performance which he at first took as an insult, but then came to regard as a compliment. He had just finished making a speech and was approached by a woman who told him that she had gone to high school with him.

"You know," she said, "you've done very well with what little you had to start with."

"I thought that was a put-down," Dr. Peale said, "but then I got to thinking about it. You know, that's really what I've been speaking about and writing about all my life."

Dr. Peale explained that after all is said and done, a person can set no finer objective than to make the most of whatever talent they possess. You don't have to be endowed with a lot of talent. Just use what you have, Dr. Peale said, and you'll go far.

It's one thing to *say* we want to perform better. It's another thing to set that as an objective and work toward it. And it's something else again to know whether we're in fact doing better.

The only way to be sure we're making any progress is to have an objective, to set goals for reaching that objective, and to measure our progress against those goals.

So, let's look at some of the basic ideas on which the *Better Makes Us Best* philosophy is built. We need to do that before we can make it work for us.

What do we mean by:

Performance
Objective
Goal
Perfection
Best
Better

Performance

> If a man is called to be a streetsweeper, he should sweep streets even as Michelangelo painted, or Beethoven composed music, or Shakespeare wrote poetry. He should sweep streets so well that all the hosts of the heaven and earth will pause to say, 'Here lived a great streetsweeper who did his job well.'
>
> Martin Luther King, Jr.

Performance is the result of our efforts.

Performance is not the effort itself, it's the product of the effort. It's how we do. Well or poorly. Quickly or slowly. On schedule or late. Successful or failed.

Whether we're secretaries or sales representatives, machine operators or managers, performance is our product.

Objective

That's our destination.

Our objective may be the place where we want to go. Our objective may be the results we want to produce.

Or, looked at in a larger sense, our objective is our own personal, never-ending quest to achieve the fullest measure of our potential. To produce our own personal best. To know whether at work, at home, or in the community, we are making the most of our lives, of ourselves.

At work, for example, our continuing objective might be to design, develop, and deliver the highest quality, most cost-effective products.

Goal

A goal is a milestone by which we mark our progress toward our objective.

A goal is a mini-objective. It tells us whether we're moving in the right direction.

As Oliver Wendell Holmes said:

> The great thing in the world is not so much where we stand but in what direction we are moving.

In order to reach our group's goal of delivering a shipment of products on or ahead of schedule to our customer, many of us will have our own individual and specific goals. Only if each of us reaches our individual goals successfully can our group attain our shared goal. And only by continuing to achieve our group goals can our organization progress toward its overall objective.

Perfection

> Do not wish to be anything but what you are, and try to be that perfectly.
>
> St. Francis De Sales

Perfection is the concept of the ideal. It is the excellence for which we continually can strive, even though we know that it's unrealistic to expect to achieve it.

But does that mean we should not strive for the very best? Louisa May Alcott has written:

> Far away there in the sunshine are my highest aspirations. I may not reach them, but I can look and see

their beauty, believe in them and try to follow where they lead.

Best

> The quality of a person's life is in direct proportion to their commitment to excellence, regardless of their chosen field of endeavor.
>
> Vince Lombardi

If it's not possible to be perfect, why not at least try to be the best?

Becoming *the* best is something that some people with intense pride in their performance set as their ultimate objective. They would pit themselves and their performance against everyone else in the world performing the same task or role.

But becoming *the* best involves the perceptions of other people, and their making judgments on our performance. That's an external evaluation and it involves measurement, which isn't always precise; and it's beyond our control. On the other hand, becoming *our* best is something within our own control and therefore within our own reach. And it's especially within our control if we seek to become our best by working each day to perform...

Better.

Better

To perform better is something that is within the reach of every one of us every day.

Perhaps performing better fills a basic human need.

We do know that when we give something our fullest effort we have that satisfied, fulfilled, and proud feeling that comes only from knowing we are making the most of our abilities and our opportunities.

That's because when we're performing better, we're moving toward our objective of getting the utmost out of our potential.

We are not stuck in a rut — instead we are propelled along in the exciting and dynamic process of *becoming* the best we can be.

General George S. Patton knew this feeling:

> Accept the challenges, so that you may feel the exhilaration of victory.

2

*Looking at the
Roadmap First*

If We Don't Know Where We're Going, How Will We Know When We Get There?

Working without having goals and objectives is like loading the luggage in the car, dropping off the dog at the kennel, pulling out onto the road — and having no idea of what our destination is. Sure, it can be fun and exciting for a while, just wandering around. But eventually not knowing where we're going gets frustrating.

So, if we're going to get anywhere, we will have to pull over to the side of the road and make up our minds just where it is we want to go. And then, if we're really determined to make progress, we'll get a map to help us get there.

When *Our* Best Is Better Than *The* Best

It's important to understand the difference between aiming to be *the* best and striving to be *our* best. *The* best compares us with everyone else. *Our* best compares our current performance to the level we can achieve when we use all of our talents.

Pushing ourselves to be *the* best can be discouraging and self-defeating. What if there are 1,000 people doing the same job and we say, "I'm going to be *the* best."

In most cases, except possibly for some athletic competitions, it is virtually impossible to demonstrate that any one person is undeniably *the* best at any one particular moment. But let's say we do become very, very good. Let's say we get to be better than 998 others. Where are we? We have become second best. Yes, we have fallen short of our objective. But have we failed? Only in terms of our own unreasonable goal.

When we recognize that important difference between *the* best and *our* best, then we are free to make the most meaningful and satisfying kind of progress, which is to try to improve our performance in comparison with our own toughest and most important competitor — ourselves.

And then we are also free to create our own personal plan, roadmap, and timetable to work toward our objective.

If We're Headed for an Island in the West, Why Are We Going North?

A sailing ship's captain knows that he's sometimes better off tacking or zig-zagging than by steering his ship straight toward his destination. It's much the same way on the journey toward our personal objectives.

Look at the athletes who have pushed beyond the old limits in their sports and attained performance levels once thought unreachable.

Nowadays, the four-minute mile is commonplace. But as recently as forty years ago, many thought it an impossible feat. Then, in 1954, Roger Bannister from England and John Landy from Australia pushed themselves and each other to a series of performances that were each slightly better than the previous one. By programmatically and painstakingly achieving each of their goals along the way, by refining seemingly insignificant techniques, by discovering their weaknesses and working on them until they became strengths, by working not only harder, but also smarter, both men reached the "impossible" goal. And both men shattered the once-impenetrable four-minute barrier.

As the great pitcher Catfish Hunter said:

Winning isn't everything. Wanting to win is.

In thousands of colleges and tens of thousands of high schools, young men and women are achieving performance levels far beyond what they might have attained a generation ago. They're able to do it not just because they are better athletes but because their coaches have learned and the athletes have learned that a person doesn't become a star overnight. For every athlete who is blessed with natural gifts, there are hundreds with ordinary skills who become fine performers through a disciplined program of achieving slightly better performance each time out.

The writer Arthur Flowers put it succinctly in his article "Playing to Win":

> Obstacles that confront you are merely challenges to your ability to grow. Invitations to power. This is the attitude of the person whose approach to life is a never-ceasing search for opportunities to grow stronger . . . To be more competent tomorrow than I am today.

So, just like the skipper with his hand on the tiller headed for an island in the west, since we can't get there all at once, we're better off to break up the trip into chunks we can manage. By successfully reaching each milepost along the way, we'll eventually make port safely.

I Don't Like Setting a Goal Because What Do I Do If I Fail to Reach It?

On September 26, 1983, Dennis Conner fell short of achieving his goal.

Conner's setback was one of the most highly publicized defeats in sports history. For when Conner's yacht *Liberty* was beaten by *Australia II*, the longest winning streak in sports history — 132 years — was snapped. The America's Cup left the United States for the first time.

Conner could have given up. In fact, a lot of people told him he should pack it in.

Instead, Dennis Conner immediately set this new goal:

TO BECOME THE FIRST AMERICAN
TO WIN BACK THE AMERICA'S CUP

And Dennis Conner set up a systematic three-and-a-half-year program of specific goals to reach that goal.

First, he assembled a group of skilled performers who knew their jobs and knew how to work together as a team.

Next, team members set goals and schedules.

Over the next 42 months, Conner and his team found ways to create just the kind of ship they would need for the waters they would encounter in the Indian Ocean, off the coast of Perth, Australia, where the America's Cup races would be held in 1986 and 1987.

Their next goal was to train a sailing crew. Then, bit by bit, they worked together to do better and better and shave fractions of a second off their times.

Finally, in February 1987, Dennis Conner and the *Stars and Stripes* team reaped the fruits of their labors. They upset a favored New Zealand ship and achieved their goal — they brought the America's Cup back from down under to the United States.

So, yes, it's okay to set a goal and come up short. If we then learn from that experience and set a new goal and a plan to reach it. Just as it's okay to make mistakes, as long as we learn from those mistakes and don't repeat them.

One of our J.P. Industries managers said it well:

One great thing about J.P. Industries is that we have the freedom to make a mistake. And, along with that,

we're also expected to have the good sense to understand that, like everyone, we will make mistakes. In
fact, if we don't come up short once in a while, we're
probably not setting our sights high enough. So it's
okay to make a mistake as long as we learn from it.

Where would we be if people were afraid to make mistakes? Still in caves. Because all important breakthroughs
come only after somebody tries to do something that has
never been done before. Surely the first person to use a ham-
mer had to suffer through a few sore thumbs before he or
she got the knack of it.

No one is immune from mistakes, not doctors, not
lawyers and not even bankers.

In June 1987, Charles Fisher III of NBD Bancorp, the
chairman and president of one of the world's largest banks,
told the National Association of Urban Banks:

> We're going to have to start to develop a culture that
> says it's OK to make mistakes. I'm not talking about
> betting the bank...I am talking about initiatives,
> trying new products, new ways of doing things.

Nowadays, sensible people realize that mistakes will happen in all areas of human endeavor. The important thing is
to get something out of the experience that will help us perform better the next time.

Look Forward Toward Where We're Going,
Not Backward Where We've Been

Some people take the attitude: "I've been doing things
the same way all my life and now I'm too set in my ways to
establish new goals and objectives."

And yet we all know of many people who started new

careers or made major breakthroughs later in life. Through-out history, many people have achieved outstanding results by setting goals and objectives and working diligently to-ward them.

The world of business and industry is full of such women and men. As are the worlds of literature, music, science, art, and sports: Grandma Moses...George Washington Carver...Andres Segovia...Pablo Picasso...George Bernard Shaw...Virginia Woolfe...the list goes on.

Elmore "Dutch" Leonard has become one of America's best-selling and most successful fiction writers. He has been on the cover of America's news magazines and has been called the nation's finest master of his trade by the *New York Times.* His books, like *Touch, Bandits, Glitz,* and *Stick,* consistently top the best-seller lists. Fourteen of his novels have either been made into feature films or are in the works, with stars like Paul Newman, Burt Reynolds, George Segal, Alan Alda, and Roy Scheider.

Leonard recalls, though, that he labored in virtual obscurity for years before he became, at age 59, "an overnight success." He points out that he just kept working every day to improve his skills and that he believed in what he was doing. But it took all those years for "the literary establishment" to recognize his skill and give his talent the recognition it deserved.

There's no point in focusing on the past. That's true whether the past is brimming with success or littered with failure.

The great pitcher Satchel Paige was able to begin his fabled major league baseball career only after he was well into his forties — an age far beyond normal retirement in that sport.

Not surprising that Satchel's motto has earned im-mortality:

Don't look back. There may be something gaining on you.

Turning Limitations into Strengths

Anyone can dream up an excuse for not doing better. After all, we all have limitations or weaknesses. That goes with being human.

But a limitation — whether real or imagined — doesn't have to keep us from performing. In fact, it can be a stimulus not only to succeed but to excel.

We've already seen that age is no barrier. Because for every child prodigy, there are many late bloomers. For every Bach or Stevie Wonder, there's a George Bernard Shaw or a Grandma Moses.

And skin color, poverty, and a physical handicap aren't necessarily reasons enough either. Look, for example, at Calvin Peete.

Cal Peete grew up in a poor black neighborhood, one of 19 children in his family.

He had a short and deformed left arm. There were no country club members in the Peete household. He did not play a round of golf until he was 23. And with those disadvantages, with almost no black role models in the field he chose, it is amazing that he not only decided to play a round of golf, he set as his objective that he would become a professional golfer!

Whether it made sense or not, being a tournament golfer is what Cal Peete wanted. And so he set that as his objective and he began to work toward it. Slowly. Painfully. Methodically.

He hit shots. Tens of thousands of shots. He got pretty good. But not good enough to suit him. He wanted to get better. So he hit more shots. Hundreds, sometimes thousands every day. Until he could hit shot after shot with uncanny accuracy.

Still, it took Cal Peete ten years to qualify for the pro circuit. He was then 33 years old — ancient by touring professional standards.

But, once on the tour, he persevered. And his determination paid off. Playing with the world's greatest players on

the world's toughest courses, Calvin Peete earned the recognition of his fellow pros and the golf galleries as one of the most precise shot-makers in the history of the game.

So, if you think you have a limitation that's keeping you from progressing, remember what Jard DeVille wrote in *Nice Guys Finish First:*

> The crucial aspect is the realization that you can shape life as you want it to become, rather than being acted upon by forces and people beyond your control.

Many people not only have overcome limitations, they have turned those limitations into strengths. Actors, athletes, artists, and others discussing their success often mention that they worked on their weaknesses until they became their strongest features.

In the words of Olympic ice dancing champions Carol Fox and Richard Dalley:

> Our biggest stumbling blocks turned into our biggest stepping stones.

In the Baseball Hall of Fame in Cooperstown, New York, there is inscribed the name of a man who was born tongue-tied. It took years of training and hard work for him to speak clearly. But eventually he succeeded so well that he became the first active announcer to be inducted into the Hall. That announcer — Ernie Harwell, who provides the play-by-play commentary for radio broadcasts of Detroit Tiger games — has spent half a century practicing a skill he learned in order to overcome an impediment.

What's Wrong with Perfection?

By definition, nothing is wrong with perfection. Perfection is the concept of the ideal toward which men and women have striven since time immemorial. Whether the person be an artist, an athlete, a lab technician, a craftsman, a machinist — or anything else — perfection in performance or execution is the ultimate desire.

But while we try to achieve it, we should not become obsessed with the pursuit of it. To see why, let's look at a parable of three young men who wanted to perform better.

A Parable

A Philosophy that Works
for
Any Tom, Dick, or Harry

Once there were three young men. They were exactly the same in almost every way.

The three young men — Tom, Dick, and Harry — were the same in looks and in age. They were the same in what they liked and didn't like. And they were exactly the same in ability.

They lived in the same town and went to the same school and when they got out of school, they each got jobs at the Little Marvel Company. They started work on the same day and they each ran exactly the same kind of machine. Their job was to make Little Marvel moldings. And each enjoyed his job and was very good at it.

One day, Tom, Dick, and Harry met for lunch and talked about how fortunate they were to have a job doing something they liked and were good at.

Tom said, "Having a job you like and are good at is great. But you know what would be terrific?

"To be the greatest maker of Little Marvel moldings in the history of all mankind. That would be just fantastic!"

Dick and Harry looked at each other. They were skeptical.

"How could you ever know you were the very best maker of moldings ever?" Dick said. "If you can't know that, then wouldn't it be unrealistic to set that as an objective?"

"I agree," Harry said. "The only way you could know that you were the greatest ever would be to be perfect. And nobody's perfect."

"Precisely!" said Tom. "No one has ever been a perfect maker of moldings. Until now. That will be my objective. To be the perfect maker of moldings!"

And he went off to make his plans to become the perfect maker of moldings.

"Isn't that something?" said Dick. "He really thinks that's an objective he can strive for — to become perfect."

"Yes," said Harry. "It's a shame, all right. Being perfect is not a realistic objective."

"No," said Dick. "What he really should have set as his objective is this: To be the very best maker of moldings who ever came down the pike. Not perfect. But the very best ever. Now there's a noble objective!"

He thrust one finger in the air. "And that's what I'm setting as my objective: To be número uno — the very best ever!"

They were silent for a moment. Finally Harry said, "I don't think that's realistic either. How can you really know for sure that you're the very best? And even if you do become the best, what do you do when someone else comes along and does it even better? Then you're no longer the best. Then what?"

Dick shook his head and laughed as he started back to his work station. He was eager to begin working toward his objective of becoming the best maker of moldings ever.

He called back over his shoulder, "I'll worry about that when the time comes. Right now this kid has only one thing in mind: To be the best."

Harry thought about it for a while. He decided that, in a way, his friends had a good idea. Yes, it is a good thing to have an objective to work toward. But to be *perfect*? To be the *very best ever*?

And it occurred to him that in this one very important way — in setting goals and objectives — he and his two friends were very different indeed.

So Harry went back to his work station and talked about it with his supervisor. When they were done talking, Harry took out a slip of paper and on it he wrote a few words. Then he went back to work.

When the sun rose the next morning, it was the first day that the three young men went to work with their new goals proudly before them.

As soon as Tom arrived at this work station, he put up a sign:

> I WILL ACCEPT NOTHING SHORT OF PERFECTION

The morning went by. Tom was indeed perfect.

"Oh, I know I'm going quite a bit slower than usual," he said to himself. "But that's okay because what I'm after is nothing less than perfection."

And he continued to turn out perfect moldings. For six hours.

Then it happened.

Despite his slow pace, he somehow made a mistake. Or the machine didn't work quite properly. Or the mixture wasn't quite right. He never knew the reason. But somehow Tom produced a molding that wasn't perfect.

He stared at the imperfect molding a long time. Then he looked at his sign:

> I WILL ACCEPT NOTHING SHORT OF PERFECTION

And Tom didn't know what to do next.

That same morning, Dick had pinned a sign to the wall at his work station. His sign said:

```
WHY NOT THE BEST?
```

He felt sorry for Tom. He knew his friend had tried so hard to be perfect. That night, he tried to console him. But when Dick went to work the next day, he was determined to continue to pursue his own objective.

A week went by. Then two.

Everyone in the plant was talking about what a terrific job Dick was doing. No one could remember anyone ever doing a better job at making moldings. So good a job did he do, that it inspired others in Dick's department to improve their performance.

Then, the third week, one of the veterans in his department tried so hard that somehow he broke all the records Dick had set. And then, a week later, a newcomer — fresh from training with new techniques — broke those records.

Dick looked at his sign. He vowed he would once again make progress toward his objective — to become the best. And once again he was making great strides — until the operator at the next station set still another record.

Two months later, Dick and all the other molding makers were exhausted and discouraged. No one could set records any more. Not only that, they couldn't even keep up with their old averages. Somehow, work wasn't very rewarding anymore.

It was many months later. Harry thought about what had happened. He still felt very badly for his two friends. And

Tom and Dick talked wistfully of the good old days when they were happy making moldings like Harry.

And they asked him how had he succeeded where they had failed.

"First," he told them, "I talked it over with my supervisor. You know, he had some good ideas. We agreed on what would be a good target for me to aim for. Then, I just worked steadily at it."

Harry told his friends that he had seen some good days and some not-so-good days. But when he came up short of a goal he didn't get discouraged. When he made mistakes, he learned from them and didn't repeat them. He had the determination to keep at it because he knew that overall he was making progress toward his objective.

And while he worked toward his objective, Harry felt good about himself and his company.

"But we had objectives, too," his friends said. "Noble objectives! And ambitious goals to reach for along the way. And still we failed. What was your objective?"

Harry pointed at his sign:

> ## TO PERFORM BETTER TODAY THAN I DID YESTERDAY

"That's it?" they said.

"Yes," he said. "That's it. It seemed to me that life is like a set of railroad tracks with lots of milestones along the way. The final destination is perfection at what you do. But it's not very realistic to become perfect, so you just keep travelling and trying. Sure, sometimes you come up short. But you learn from your mistakes and your experiences."

"How do you know when you've arrived?" Tom said.

"Yes," Dick added, "how can you tell when you've reached your objective?"

Harry smiled. "Well, you don't actually ever reach your objective. You just keep trying. And you keep getting closer and better, but never really arriving."

"But isn't that frustrating?" Tom wondered, "Doesn't it bother you to know you'll never get to a final place where you know you can't get any better?"

Harry thought about it.

He looked at his sign and then he looked at Tom and Dick.

"Well, at first I thought that, too. Then I discovered something that works — at least it works for me," he said.

"What counts is that I'm becoming a little bit better as I go along the way. That my life is under my own control and I'm becoming the best that I can be. I'm also learning to feel better about myself and working toward my potential."

Tom and Dick looked at each other. Then they looked at Harry. And the three of them smiled. Once again they were alike — they agreed on what was important and how to strive for it.

3

Getting There by Goal Setting

People Are Only Human

It's important to keep human nature in mind. We often tend to set goals beyond our reach. Studies of goal setting by individuals and groups have shown again and again that it's frustrating and even self-defeating to set unrealistically high goals. So, people who set goals that are far too high and then fall short of them often give up. That's easy to understand. People don't like to fail, so instead of lowering our goals to a realistic and achievable level, we abandon them.

We don't want people at J.P. Industries to be turned off and burned out because of trying to be perfect and coming up short. Indeed, no matter where you work, you shouldn't have to experience such frustration.

Instead, you want to feel the satisfaction that comes from knowing you're growing, improving, and making more of your talents and opportunities.

But — it's just as important not to underestimate yourself by setting goals that are beneath your ability.

Lecturer Larry Bielat put it this way:

> Unless you try to do something beyond what you have already done and mastered, you will never grow.

And Charles Garfield, in his book *Peak Performers: The New Heroes of American Business*, said:

> Peak performers are made, not born. This may seem like an obvious point, yet it is one that numerous

people fail to grasp. I have found that the average person can accomplish 40 to 50 percent more than he thinks he can.

What's important is that you set your goals neither too high nor too low. Too high and you set yourself up for failure, too low and you fail to achieve your personal best. So, goal setting is one of the most important, personal, and individual decisions you can make.

When you yourself help determine the next goal you will work toward in your quest to improve your performance, you have a personal stake in that goal. If you have a stake in a goal, if you feel that it is within your power and ability to achieve it, you feel more strongly committed to working to attain it.

But when a quota has been imposed on you by others it's natural that you don't feel as personally dedicated to achieving it.

As you set goals and objectives, you should keep in mind the two extremes.

On the one hand, you shouldn't be too timid, because as lecturer Robert N. Coons put it:

IF THE SHOE FITS, YOU'RE NOT ALLOWING FOR GROWTH

But on the other hand, as you've seen, having an objective of "being the best" can be unrealistic and frustrating. Somewhere in the middle is having an objective of "performing better today than I did yesterday." That's realistic, personally fulfilling, action-oriented, and dynamic.

An Idea That Works for Everyone

The *Better Makes Us Best* approach is not something that's available to just a privileged few. The opposite is true — it's something to which each person can relate. And it is near at hand, not distant. It is personal, not generalized and abstract.

But even though being better begins as a personal and individual commitment, a very interesting thing can happen within an organization filled with people who work each day toward individual and personal goals of performing better than they did the day, or the week, or the year before. That organization can progress toward becoming the best that it can be. Whether it's the best of its kind is less important.

Just saying the words, "I want to be the best," can't achieve this kind of progress. But working each day to be better can. This is the premise and the power of the philosophy, *Better Makes Us Best*.

By striving to perform better each day than you did the day before, and by setting realistic, attainable, and yet worthy goals, you can be more successful and more fulfilled. Goals stimulate you to move forward. Goals are the yardstick by which you measure your growth and performance.

How to Get Started

The first thing is not to make a big production out of getting started. It isn't like quitting smoking or going on a diet — that involves changing basic habits or living patterns.

Instead, what you'll find is that you're really not giving up something. You're adding something.

When you make the decision that you want the things that come from performing better, you're adding something new to your life, something of your own choice. That's important. You're personally setting forth what you

want to work toward. And you yourself are deciding on the goals by which you will chart your progress toward your objectives.

Some companies have elaborate systems with titles like, "Maximizing Employee Skill Potential through Systematic Attainment of Quantifiable and Incremental Periodic Performance Attainment Levels."

In plain English that means: "Getting more out of your job by having goals."

And in many organizations there are thick manuals and video modules and cassette tapes explaining the goals and objectives program. There are yards of forms to be filled out. And, of course, there are workshops explaining how to fill out the forms.

By the time people have spent hours in those sessions, and more hours reading and filling out forms, whatever vitality there might have been has been bled dry. Finally, people say the heck with it — they're too worn out or bored to care much about reaching some quota that was probably determined by their boss or their boss' boss anyhow.

That sort of an approach is no fun. It wastes time. It turns people off instead of turning them on. And one more thing — it doesn't work.

So we don't intend to use that approach at J.P. Industries as we work toward being better. We simply want to make it easy, enjoyable, and more worthwhile for people to do it than not to do it. We believe that if we try to do better, it will work for us. And we believe that what works for each of us works for the good of our whole company.

There's a sign posted in the basketball locker room at the University of Michigan:

COMING TOGETHER IS A BEGINNING,
KEEPING TOGETHER IS PROGRESS,
WORKING TOGETHER IS SUCCESS

If you watched Michigan's basketball team win the 1989 NCAA championship, you witnessed a striking example of what can happen when people in a group work *together* to be the best they can be.

You're the Expert

The first thing you need before you can set your objectives and goals is an understanding of your job. You have to know what makes for acceptable performance and what is very good performance and what is outstanding performance. And you *do* know those things because each of you should be the expert on your own job.

But how do you turn that knowledge into goal-setting?

Well, you should think about how well you performed when you were at the top of your game. What had you accomplished by the end of one of your very best days? What had you designed, or produced, or delivered, or sold in your all-time best week?

Should you set that as your goal for your everyday or every week performance?

Before answering that question, suppose for a moment you are a salesman who in a typical week averages ten orders totaling a thousand units sold. Then once, in your best week, you wrote up *twenty* orders totaling *two* thousand units. Should you set an annual objective based on being able to repeat that single outstanding week fifty times? Should twenty orders and two thousand units be your new weekly goal?

Not unless you want to become very, very frustrated.

But should you instead settle for turning in the same kind of numbers year after year, maybe with a two or three percent improvement?

Not unless you want to admit that you haven't learned much or gained in ability in the past year. Not unless you want to admit to yourself you have reached your ultimate level of performance. That you don't want the feeling of satisfaction that comes from discovering your potential and making the most of it.

Instead, here's a process I'd suggest can be followed successfully by anyone.

First Step

Determine your objective and goals.

Knowing what you do about your job, what would be the level you would feel good about reaching? That's your objective. For example, if you are in sales, you might look at a sales increase the same as the inflation rate as "just treading water." You may feel really good if you increase your sales every year more than that. *You* set the objective. The important thing is to know the direction you want to go.

Then, set your goals.

Your goals are stepping stones on the way to your objective. They will help you determine how fast you're going to get there.

Set performance targets that you know from the past are just within reach of your fingertips — but not within easy grasp. Remember, to feel good about yourself, you need to stretch. But don't "set yourself up" for failure.

Goal setting takes practice. Sometimes it's useful to think about all the things you could do to improve your performance and estimate how much difference each change would make.

Prioritizing is important. Look to see if it makes sense to make changes in a particular order, or to make small changes first.

But do decide what changes to make and how much of a difference you would expect. And set some time limits for yourself.

Second Step

Once you have your objectives and goals penciled down, go over them with your supervisor or boss.

And it's important that you do it in that order — objectives first, *then* talk with the boss.

If your boss comcs to you first with numbers he or she wants to shoot for, just say that you need a little time to come up with your own numbers.

Then, once you have your own ideas in mind, talk with your boss, show what you've drafted and see how that compares with what your boss thinks. After all, these are numbers you will both be working with. And you both have to be comfortable with them.

We've talked about goals expressed in numbers. Actually, objectives and goals don't always have to be numbers. But they do always have to be stated in specific measurable terms.

Why is that?

Because otherwise you'll never really know whether or not you're making progress.

And, for the same reason, you'll need to have milestone dates, too. An open-ended goal is a moving target — it isn't really something you can set your sights on.

Third Step

Put it on paper.

Put it on the wall, if you want. Or on a card on your desk. Or on a slip of paper you carry in your wallet or purse. Whatever you like. But it's a good idea to keep your goals in a place where you'll see them frequently.

It won't be long until you've totally committed them to memory.

You may find that unlike some lofty New Year's resolutions, your own personal goals and objectives for your job will be something you will continue to be aware of and care about and work to achieve.

Be sure to work each day on meeting your goal. Check every so often to see if you should raise your sights or lower them. Ask for feedback. Look for ways to focus your energy and effort to meet your goal.

Target your efforts wherever you can. That's the best reason you have for measuring performance.

Remember, as Detroit television personality John Gross said:

> Setting goals and not acting on them is like making a cake and then not putting it in the oven.

But What If We Come Up Short?

It's natural to wonder, "What happens if I can't achieve my goals?"

Well, first of all, the world won't come to an end.

But you will need to determine why you didn't achieve them. Maybe the goals were too ambitious. You'll probably already know the answer to that or will be able to come up with an explanation you're comfortable with by talking it over with your boss.

If your goals were too ambitious, look for ways to trim them into smaller pieces. If you hit roadblocks, look for ways to work around them. It's important not to just give up.

Remember, you've probably accomplished a lot already just because you tried. So you should be proud of what you've achieved.

However, it may be that you reached your goals too easily. And that may mean that you didn't ask enough of yourself. Should you be content with goals you don't have to stretch to attain?

If your performance is too far off the mark in relation to your goals — whether short or long — the wisest thing you can do is re-examine and adjust your goals.

What Really Counts

Success is a journey, not a destination.

A writer named Ben Sweetland wrote those words. I agree with him.

Remember, just as the concept *Better Makes Us Best* is a dynamic one, so too is the setting of objectives and goals. Having specific objectives and goals is not an end in itself, it's a means to an end.

The purpose is not to see who is the best person at setting goals by gearing your performance to match those pre-set goals. The idea is instead to have something specific you're trying to achieve and a sense of direction. What you're really seeking is that matchless feeling of growing, improving, and getting ever closer to becoming your personal best.

You may find that you revise your goals several times in a few months. If so, that's fine. Many a successful person has said, "Getting there was more fun than being there." That's because one of life's greatest satisfactions comes from pushing yourself to discover the boundaries of your abilities.

Pro tennis champion Martina Navratilova knows that feeling well:

> I've learned over the years that if I say, 'I'm going to win Wimbledon, and that will make me happy,' it won't work. It just doesn't work that way. That kind of high can be over in a day or two. What I've learned to enjoy is the getting there, the working out.

And imagine how enjoyable it is to be part of a group filled with people all trying to achieve their personal best.

4

Back to the Basics

Many members of the J.P. Industries work family have told me about their personal experiences in putting the *Better Makes Us Best* philosophy into action in their work lives.

In fact, I've long since stopped being surprised at how well our people have made it work. And I always am pleased to hear how someone has made our philosophy work not only on the job, but in other areas.

That's why I'm always glad to hear about someone's personal experience in achieving exciting new goals by using this approach.

Not long ago, one of our J.P. Industries managers wrote something that reminded me again how frequently we fail to see the most simple and obvious truths. Here's what that manager said:

> Better Makes Us Best is a philosophy that I will not only use in my daily job, but in my personal life with my family. I believe that if children adopt this attitude of continuing their efforts and striving to be better, they will achieve their own personal best no matter what they are participating in.

This is an example of the importance of fundamental truths and values in our lives. Here is a conscientious and dedicated person who has found a surge of new purpose by going back to the basics.

It didn't have to be the *Better Makes Us Best* concept. It could just as well have been something else. But what's important is the reminder that we would do well in our fast-paced, sophisticated, high-tech society to revisit the fundamentals from time to time. What we're talking about is a system of growth that is balanced. Companies, as well as people, need to have a healthy way of growing.

The frontiers of knowledge are being pushed out so swiftly that, in an effort to keep up with alarmingly rapid progress, we are in grave danger of leaving some very good things behind. We should be concerned that so many of our computer-literate children cannot add a simple column of numbers. We should be concerned that the increasing emphasis on computer monitors linked to electronic data bases may produce a generation of young people who are uncomfortable with a book in their hands.

It is because of these concerns that I was surprised, pleased, and personally grateful to hear that at least one of our people had discovered that if *Better Makes Us Best* works on the job, it might just work in other parts of his life.

If we can perform better as parents, as members of our communities, so much the better. The same principles would seem to apply, wouldn't they?

Can anyone be the *perfect* mother? Or the *best* of all fathers? And how could one become the *perfect* community member, or the *best* citizen? Those are simply not realistic objectives. But to be a *better* parent, a *better* neighbor today than we were last week, yes, that is within our reach, within our power.

And it pleases me when our fellow employees at J.P. Industries remind us of that simple and important truth.

The Power of a Simple Idea

The very simplicity of the concept may be a reason why it has not yet become more popular in our culture.

In our modern societies, the sophisticated, the esoteric, and the convoluted often seem to be more in vogue than the simple, the basic, and the straightforward. Thus we frequently have government productivity experts and industry analysts talking about "the efficacies of Japanese-style management techniques in a U.S. plant environment." Or scholars debating whether "Theory X is more plausible than Theory Y for making America competitive again in the world marketplace."

Not that it isn't important to try to understand better the dynamics of the workplace, the elements of the work experience, and how we can become more successful and thereby happier and more productive at our jobs.

But we shouldn't let that distract us from the basics. For to do that is to make the same mistake made by so many before us, which is to overlook the power of a simple idea.

Let our experts look for the subtleties and nuances in how to improve our performance. And when they discover them, let's learn from them. When they have a new insight or make a breakthrough, let's take what works and incorporate it into our factories and offices.

But in the meantime, let's take full advantage of the simple but powerful lesson we have already learned at J.P. Industries.

That lesson is that you *get* better by *trying* and *performing* better.

Do we ever become so good that we can be content with our performance? Not if we believe champion pro golfer Fuzzy Zoeller:

> I'm always out there trying to learn something different. If you consider yourself a great player, where do you go from there?

Better is as better does. Each person, each day. Not startling productivity increases by super heroes. Just solid, steady improvement like Harry in the parable in Chapter Two. And by average men and women who understand and are committed to the concept *Better Makes Us Best.*

5

Communication:
The Lifeblood of
a Successful Company

The rapid changes that take place in modern society demand that more people know more about more things. And that they learn it much faster than ever before.

As a result, we communicate with each other more frequently and about a wider variety of things. And the amount, speed, and varieties of communication grow greater every day. As we communicate more, it's also essential that we communicate better, because more people are affected by and have to know about changes, new ideas, and developments.

That is not to say that people today are necessarily more intelligent or better educated than previous generations. But you and I are exposed to much more information than our parents were. And in order to do our jobs and grow, we have to be able to communicate effectively. That means both taking in and giving out information. That means sharing ideas and information with fellow workers who need it to do their job. That means being accurate when we inform others. And prompt in sharing that information when timeliness is important.

At J.P. Industries, we make a distinction between information flow and decision making based on that information. That's because we have to have an environment in which information can be openly and easily shared with those who need it to do their job. We have to be able to communicate information with different kinds of people in various situations. But we do not want to set up conflicting actions.

We need to be able to go to the person in the organization who has the information we need, regardless of either person's rank. And, unless that information is confidential or can't be disclosed for legitimate reasons, the information should be shared. We have to be perfectly free to ask for information that we need to perform our job or to be as effective as possible in our work team. Not only that, we should understand that if we are to bring forth our best we should energetically seek to know and understand more. And, of course, it also follows that we should be forthcoming when others request information from us. Only in this way can an idea stay alive and have a chance to grow.

However, that does *not* mean that anyone can make a decision or take any action she or he may think appropriate based on that information. There is a difference between information channels and decision channels. The first is informal, unstructured and knowledge-oriented. It sparks ideas and suggestions. The second is formal, more structured and action-oriented. It triggers decisions and authorizes actions. Thus everyone can move smoothly ahead together.

Good ideas often have difficulty surviving in troubled organizations. In those settings, the atmosphere is such that people are not encouraged to bring forward their ideas.

"We already know all the answers," is the attitude. Actually, in organizations that are having problems, the opposite is often true. There are two important things wrong about thinking that "We already know all the answers."

First, *no one* knows all the answers.

Second, frequently those people who think they know the right answers don't even know enough to ask the right questions.

Moreover, in unhealthy organizations, people are often afraid of new ideas and new information — afraid that it will change their role, their power.

Compare that with a successful organization, where new ideas represent opportunities for everyone to grow. Here, the philosophy is instead:

We'll take good ideas wherever we can get them. A good idea doesn't care where it came from.

A common feature of a healthy company is that people are well aware that they don't know all the answers. Good managers, particularly, know that each employee is far more knowledgeable than the bosses ever could be about the details of their jobs. These managers know that if their work group is going to improve its performance, it will take more than just hard work. It will take a constant infusion of fresh input from the people who are actually closest to the task.

And it will take the freedom to ask the dumb question.

The Freedom to Ask the Dumb Question

"What would happen if the earth really isn't flat and you sailed west from Spain..."

"What would happen if you could cultivate a yeast mold like the kind that grows on bread and you could inject it in people with certain kinds of infections and..."

Many great advances have come about only because someone was not afraid to ask "the dumb" question.

About twenty years ago, Martin Allen looked at a display of George Washington's tools at the Smithsonian Institution. It occurred to him that there had been very little change in drafting equipment in two centuries. So he asked a dumb question: "Why not teach a computer what it needs to know to help engineers do product design?"

His "dumb" idea was that he could use technology to improve on techniques that designers had apparently been doing quite well with for centuries. His objective was to free designers from the centuries-old but laborious task of modifying their visual displays on their drawing board or a hard model. Instead they could actually manipulate a visual display. This would greatly shorten developmental cycles.

reduce costs, and bring new products out faster. A lot of people thought this was a stupid idea. After all, engineering had been done the same way for ages, hadn't it?

But from this "dumb" question was born the technology of computer-aided design/computer-aided manufacturing, or CAD/CAM.

Big Ideas Come in All Sizes

At J.P. Industries, we're proud of our employees who have come up with productive and ingenious ideas such as those that have made possible improvements in quality or delivery schedules or reductions in scrap. We've featured some of these employees and their ideas in our annual report and other communications. We'll continue to acknowledge this kind of initiative and independent thinking. With the competitive pressures we face, we need breakthrough thinking like that.

What's important is that we value every idea — there are no small ideas.

And that's where a subtle but important part of communication comes in. I'm talking about creating the kind of environment in which ideas can sprout and flourish. Ideas are fragile. Especially breakthrough ideas. Many brilliant ideas undoubtedly sounded ridiculous the first time someone else heard them. There is no such thing as a bad time or place to have a good idea. Not if you have the gift of curiosity.

The Gift of Curiosity

Can you imagine getting an idea that spawns an entire industry while you're brushing your dog's coat?

George de Mestral was intrigued about something which countless people had grumbled about and never paid much attention to. He noticed how stubborn the burrs were when he tried to brush them out of his dog's coat. So, he looked at them through a microscope. What he saw was hundreds of tiny hooks. And what was born was the idea for the Velcro fastener.

Do we want blockbuster ideas at J.P. Industries? Sure we do. But an idea doesn't have to be an industry-changing innovation to be meaningful.

What we are trying to encourage at our company is a climate in which fresh ideas can get a thoughtful hearing. And, if they have merit, can flourish.

It isn't always possible to implement a seemingly exciting new process or to make adjustments in workways that find all parties "winning." But it is a lot more likely to happen in an atmosphere of open communication and shared commitment to common goals.

There are many organizations — far too many — in which employees would not come forward because they had been discouraged from doing so in the past. Because they would fear their ideas would be rejected out of hand. Because they would know their management is not receptive to any ideas except their own.

In some cases, employees don't communicate their ideas out of a concern that to do so would mean "end-running my boss...going outside of authorized communication lines... muddying the waters by not going through proper channels."

Those are very legitimate concerns. Once an organization reaches a certain size, it's important that it establish procedures and systems for getting decisions communicated. As a company grows, there are more people and more functions, and there has to be a set of procedures and a discipline for conducting business and making decisions.

But we must not let systems and procedures become an end in themselves. When that happens, it hurts our ability to adapt and to make necessary changes.

So, what we expect of our managers at J.P. Industries is to maintain the delicate balance we need between the entrepreneurial "free spirit" approach and the discipline needed to bring good ideas to market.

Clear Communication (Information vs. Decision)

I have found many times that when information is not shared directly, one on one, it changes after it leaves the originator. Ideas get filtered. The clarity of the original thought goes out of focus. The power is lost. Or, where there should be cooperation, instead there is an element of politics.

And there goes the enthusiasm of the person with the idea.

An organization that encourages widespread one-on-one communication and keeps that enthusiasm for new ideas alive is a vibrant, enjoyable organization.

But I learned several years ago that you do have to be careful about communicating clearly whether you are asking for information only or whether you are asking for action to carry out a decision.

At the time, before we started J.P. Industries, I was chief technical officer of another company. While walking around the factory floor, I was curious about the location of a large and impressive machine that had just been installed. It was not my area of expertise or responsibility and I just wondered why it was located where it was. So I asked the foreman of the operation, "Why is that machine set up here, instead of, say, over there?"

He went to great pains to explain what a big and expensive project it had been to install that machine there. He actually told me far more than I cared to know. But his explanation made sense and, my curiosity satisfied, I thanked him and left.

Two weeks later, I visited that location again. I was surprised to notice that the machine I had inquired about the last time was no longer there — it had been moved to another location. I spotted the foreman and asked him about it. "Well, you didn't want it set up where it was," he said. "So we moved it."

Now, I had not thought for a moment that I was giving directions to that foreman. I had merely wondered out loud about something. I had been seeking information. He had provided it.

But I had also mistakenly communicated something else in the process. I had somehow given the impression I was directing action — that I wanted a machine moved, at considerable effort and expense. And I often have wished that the foreman had asked me the "dumb" question: Why did I want that done?

Since then, I have always kept in mind the element of unintended communication. It is the responsibility of the person doing the talking to be very sure that his or her intended message is coming through, but more than that, that other messages are not unintentionally coming through.

It's one thing to seek or gather information in order to understand something better. It's another to make and communicate a decision. We have to know how to do both. And we have to be careful that we and others are clear on what we're doing.

Anyone Can Discover the Secret Ingredient

Another important aspect of communication is the responsibility of an individual member of a group to come forward with information important to the successful operation of the group.

An industrial consultant once gave me an example of how anyone can have a piece of information that can make an important difference. Sometimes the difference may seem small — but sometimes it may mean the success or failure of a company.

The consultant explained that there once was a man who owned a hog farm and knew very little about the details of the operation. The owner was alarmed when he noticed that more than 50 percent of the piglets were dying in the first few weeks after birth. When this trend continued, it was clear that the financial health of the business was in jeopardy. So, he called in experts to find the cause.

Nutrition experts analyzed the food. Environmental experts did exhaustive checks on the air, water, and soil. Veterinarians were instructed to take tissue samples and look for rare diseases.

No one could find the explanation. The high death rate continued and it looked as if the operation would go under.

One day, an old farm hand who had worked in the place for years showed up at the owner's office. He was dressed in his work overalls and was uncomfortable. He obviously was regretting he had come forward. Although he had something to tell the owner, he was clearly afraid that by talking about a problem, he would get blamed for it.

The owner could see the man's discomfort. He tried to reassure the man. He told him that he could speak freely and say what was on his mind.

"It's about those piglets," he said. "The ones that are dying."

"Yes," the owner said. "And if it keeps up at this rate, we'll be out of business. I've had all the experts in and no one knows the reason."

The farm hand was silent for a time.

"Well, I know the reason."

"You do? What is it?"

"Well, we used to move the piglets away from the sows at night. Then a few months ago, someone told us not to bother doing that."

The owner was puzzled. "What's that got to do with our problem?"

"At night is when it happens," the farm hand said. "The sows roll over on the little fellows and they can't get any air. They suffocate."

The old farm hand had known the reason all along but had been afraid to go against what he thought were orders from on high. And he hesitated saying anything about it out of fear that he himself could get blamed.

We live in a complex and sophisticated society in which there are far more opportunities for things to go wrong than there are on a hog farm. As robots and sophisticated machines do more and more of our physical labor, it becomes increasingly important that each of us bring forth not only our personal best efforts, but also the information that will help others to do their jobs. The result will be to preserve the health of the entire organization of which we are a part.

Effective communication is essential to achieving our full potential and enjoying our work life to the fullest. We need to have the information we require to do our jobs. And we need to share information if we are to be as successful as we want to be.

So, at J. P. Industries, our managers try their best to foster an environment in which there is a free flow of necessary information.

6

Growth, Change and Opportunity

We recently commissioned a survey to better understand what important audiences thought about our company. While we felt we had a pretty good idea of what people thought of J.P. Industries, we needed to get unbiased and objective information to guide our strategic planning process.

One of the audiences surveyed was the financial community. Brokers, analysts, and others in the business sector told us a great deal. As one part of the survey, they shared their perceptions of the traits that came to mind when they thought of J.P. Industries. They said they thought our company was: "dynamic ... growing ... action-oriented ... evolving ... expanding ... "

There is one common thread that runs through those traits and the other traits that have been key to the growth and success of J.P. Industries ... change.

Speaking of the changes occurring at the beginning of the second half of the twentieth century, Charles de Gaulle said:

> It so happens that the world is undergoing a transfor-
> mation to which no change that has yet occurred can
> be compared, either in scope or in rapidity.

There is no question that we live in a rapidly changing world. Virtually every day there is a major technological advancement or development which has serious impact on life. That was not the case in the past. Our acceptance of that fact, our ability not only to endure change but to take advantage of it, to thrive on it, is essential to our success.

As Harvard business professor Ted Levitt has said:

> The future belongs to people who see possibilities before they become obvious.

I personally think that change and variety are exciting. It seems to me much more interesting to live in times like these that are full of new developments, new stimulations, and new opportunities.

One of our managers put it this way:

> We must get people to see beyond problems, to see the future in terms of the opportunities it will offer, not the obstacles.

There is no question that there is a price we have to pay for living in a constantly changing world: There is less tranquility, security, and predictability than there used to be. And not only are things continuing to change, the rate of change itself is accelerating.

But need we really fear forces that are beyond our control? Or should we instead accept their existence and learn to live with them?

Financier W. Clement Stone has been one of the world's most successful businessmen. He recalls coming to terms with his fear of forces beyond his control:

> I got my first lesson in overcoming fear when I was a child. I was so frightened during thunderstorms that I hid under the bed. But one day it occurred to me that if lightning should strike, it would be just as dangerous under the bed as it would be in any other part of the room. When my next opportunity came to face up to a thunderstorm, I forced myself to go to the window and look out at the lightening. An amazing thing happened: I began to enjoy the beauty of the flashes of light. By taking action, I neutralized my fear.

Rapid Change in Modern Society

What is different about change in our era is not its presence but its *pace* — the rapidity with which ideas arise, are developed and applied, and the immediacy and degree of their impact on our lives.

When I came to the United States in 1951, it was at the dawn of a new age. We didn't know it then, but we were soon to learn. A fantastic new machine had been developed. This miraculous new machine could process enormous quantities of information. It could make calculations far more quickly than any human brain. Not only that, it could perform its functions with perfect accuracy.

Even though this incredible device could do the work of a the whole department of mathematicians and in a fraction of the time, it could be fit into one large room. Of course, it cost millions of dollars, but that seemed a small price for such a powerful and marvelous thing.

Surely many people hearing about this great technological development were convinced that modern man had pushed the frontiers of science and engineering to their very limits. How could you possible improve on this all-electronic system, known then as ENIAC — which stands for Electronic Numerical Integrator and Calculator.

Soon we started calling this marvel, and its many generations of successors, by another name: the computer.

It took almost 14 centuries to progress from the invention of paper to the Gutenberg printing press. It took just four centuries to move from Gutenberg's hand-carved, hand-set type to the linotype machine. And it has taken just half a century from the first conception of the large-scale digital computer in 1937 to the wide use of personal computers by both business and individuals today. That's acceleration!

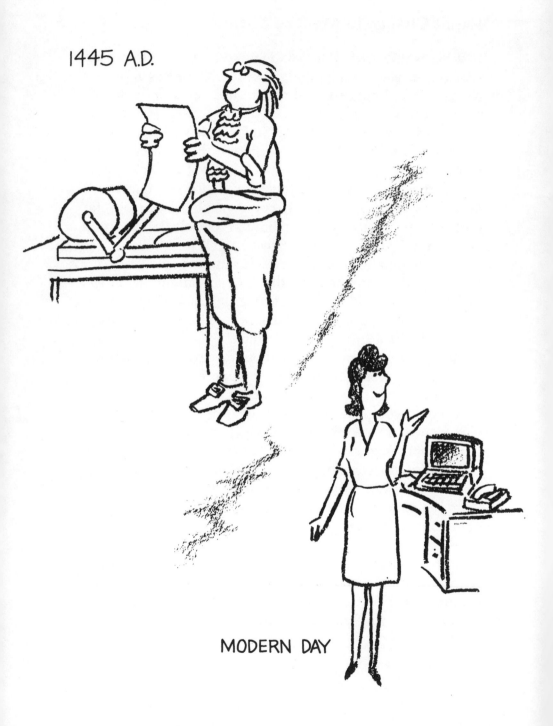

1445 A.D.

MODERN DAY

Moving Forward with Change

For better or worse, whether we like it or not, we will live out our lives in an ever-changing environment.

Despite progress in many aspects of civilization, people have historically found change uncomfortable and even threatening.

Change, especially rapid change, is often associated with disruption of stability. To most people, stability usually means security, dependability and order — all highly prized. To them, change tends to mean insecurity, uncertainty and disorder — and so they see change as a negative.

Examples of disruption due to change are all around us. A familiar instance is job security. Until fairly recently, a job with some of our larger companies was considered a lifetime employment guarantee. Today, many of these jobs are being shifted from these companies to their suppliers or other industrial sectors due to technological and competitive changes.

However positive and productive the ultimate position may be, the change itself can be upsetting, particularly when one is not anticipating and taking appropriate action such as *training*. Furthermore, it's being said that the average worker starting today will change jobs at least five times and perhaps even change fields more than once in his or her career.

Rapid change often means increased stress — both physical and psychological. The on-going adjustment to new situations, the constant demand to master new skills, the increased need to plan for a future that is less clear if not less bright, are all part of this pressure.

Moreover, it's often said that technological change — in particular the introduction of computers — can have a wide variety of negative effects. Some are personal issues such as tension from learning and adapting to new, unfamiliar and more complex equipment, or vision fatigue from constant use of computer video screens. And there are the wider concerns for society such as unemployment, invasion of individual privacy, computer crime, and breaches of security.

But despite these drawbacks, *rapid change is here to stay.* Our challenge is to learn how to meet rapid change effectively.

In such a climate, the first step is simply to accept change as a matter of course. Those who fail to accept change will slide backwards. The ones who succeed will be those who move forward with change.

Security in an Era of Change

What can we do to overcome our own internal resistance to change? We can view change as an opportunity rather than an obstacle. That is positive mental attitude at work. When we look at how we can do better whatever we are doing, we begin to take our future into our own hands. And then we begin to set the stage for greater satisfaction in our endeavors.

Self-reliance is important, as is positive thinking. Where would we be if we put too much stock in negative thinking? In 1895, Lord Kelvin, President of the Royal Society, said:

Heavier than air flying machines are impossible.

And in 1898, Charles H. Duell, Director of the U.S. Patent Office, said:

Everything that can be invented has been invented.

Fortunately some other people were looking at things positively.

A positive attitude can help prepare us for change and that in turn can mean security for the future. That's because in the world of tomorrow, security will be more under the control of the individual than ever before. Instead of being wrapped in a blanket of security provided by outside elements, the individual will make his or her own security.

That security will come from becoming a better performer
— and a better performer will be a more valued and re-
warded performer.

In fact, the new foundation on which security will be
built will be precisely that — performance.

One of our J.P. Industries employees said it this way:

> People used to talk about 'growing in their job'. But
> there's more to it than that. What you want to do is to
> grow your job. And grow along with it. And then
> grow out of your job. You'll find that the next one
> will be even more exciting and rewarding.

I agree with that.

Those of us who develop new skills and abilities will find
new opportunities open to us. We will find new ways to become even more valuable performers. And we will create
our own security.

So, far from being a threat, change is the ally of the
quick, resourceful, and dedicated performer.

And since that's the kind of people we want and need at
J.P. Industries, we look forward to change.

It will only make us better.

And better makes us best.

Acknowledgements

Many people contributed in many ways to this book. Some helped directly in the development of the manuscript. Others contributed by providing the examples that inspired the concept that is the foundation for this book, the inspirations that stimulated us to press onward, the counsel that helped shape the theory, and the criticism that challenged our theses and brought our philosophy into focus.

The limitations of space prohibit naming all, but some deserve special mention including our directors, who were present at the birth of the company and have participated in its leadership: Marvin L. Huston, Lothar Goiny, and Reid White; our current and former officers of the company, who have joined the firm at various times from its inception through 1986 and have contributed substantially to its growth: John L. Menson II, Gareth L. Reed, LeRoy W. Ranney III, Katherine M. Erdman, Richard J. Puricelli, Miguel A. Nistal, and J.H. Huss; and Nora Fileccia, an early office staff member.

Our friends at National Bank of Detroit had confidence in us and supported us from the very beginning.

Charles Hughes, founder and principal of the Center for Values Research in Dallas, Texas, helped crystallize the thoughts that would eventually be expressed in these pages.

Special contributions were made by Katherine M. Erdman, our former Vice President for Communications who is presently studying for her MBA at Boston College and Patricia B. Weber, Associate Dean, School of Business, Eastern Michigan University, and Director of the Center for Entrepreneurship. They served as sounding boards for helping develop the *Better Makes Us Best* concept into this book, and they made insightful contributions to this volume.

Others contributed their special expertise to the many processes involved in the creation and physical production of this book. John Martin drew the illustrations. Bob Ketelhut saw to the execution of the design. Joyce Ward keyboarded the manuscript and Gavin Marks oversaw the preparation of photocomposition.

Bill Haney orchestrated the process of making the book happen and guided it along the way. His assistance was invaluable in expressing the concept in the most effective way to our employee family.

Jeanne Jandron, my executive secretary, has done a stellar job helping to keep our corporate house in order and serving as a liaison between us and our friends at Productivity Press.

To these people and to the many others who contributed in essential ways to the *Better Makes Us Best* concept and to this book, my heartfelt thanks.

About the Author

Born on the Island of Crete in 1932, Psarouthakis immigrated to the United States in 1952 and attended Massachusetts Institute of Technology, earning bachelor's and master's degrees in mechanical engineering. He holds a Ph.D. in mechanical engineering from the University of Maryland and attended a program for executives at Carnegie-Mellon University.

Prior to founding J.P. Industries in 1978, Psarouthakis was employed by Boston Edison; Martin Marietta/Thermo Electron Corp.; Allis Chalmers as director of the Technology Center, new products planning and market research; and MASCO Corp. as corporate vice president for planning and technology and group vice president.

Psarouthakis is an active supporter of higher education, particularly at Eastern Michigan University, where he gave the commencement address and received an honorary Doctor of Business Administration degree in 1988. He is the founding chairman of EMU's Center for Entrepreneurship Advisory Board; a member of the College of Business Development Board and its first chairman; and former chairman of the Planning Committee for EMU's Presidents' Forum. He is a member of the Research and Development Advisory Committee for the Strategic Fund of Michigan; he serves on the Board of Trustees and is a member of the Business Advisory Council at Carnegie-Mellon; is a member of the Visiting Committee at the University of Michigan School of Business Administration; and is also a member of the Development Committee for MIT Corp.

Psarouthakis has lectured extensively on energy conversion, management, business planning, and financing and starting a business. He has published articles on management, energy conversion, electrical transmission, metal forming, and physics.

Starting with the Distinguished Young Scientist Award in 1965 from the Maryland Academy of Science, Psarouthakis has been recognized throughout his career for his contributions to his field. His most recent awards, in addition to the honorary degree from EMU, include: The MIT Corporate Leadership Award in 1987, the Medallion for Entrepreneurship by Beta Gamma Sigma National Honor Society of Schools of Business for 1988, and Entrepreneur of the Year by the Harvard Business School Alumni Club of Detroit in 1987.

Dr. John Psarouthakis

OTHER BOOKS AVAILABLE FROM PRODUCTIVITY PRESS

Productivity Press publishes and distributes materials on productivity, quality improvement, and human resource development for business and industry, academia, and the general market. Many products are direct source materials from Japan that have been translated into English for the first time and are available exclusively from Productivity. Supplemental services include conferences, seminars, in-house training programs, and industrial study missions. Send for our free book catalog.

The Eternal Venture Spirit
An Executive's Practical Philosophy
by Kazuma Tateisi

Like human health, organizational health depends on discovering the causes of symptoms that indicate an imbalance in the system. Tateisi, founder and CEO of Omron Industries, one of Japan's leading electronics companies, analyzes the signals of "big business disease" and how to respond to them so that technological innovation and entrepreneurial spirit can thrive as the organization grows and the market changes. An outstanding book on long-term strategic management, with practical benefits to everyone in the organization.
ISBN 0-915299-55-0 / 208 pages / $19.95 / Order code EVS-BK

The Idea Book
Improvement Through Total Employee Involvement
edited by the Japan Human Relations Association

What would your company be like if each employee — from line workers to engineers to sales people — gave 100 ideas every year for improving the company? This handbook of Japanese-style suggestion systems (called "teian"), will help your company develop its own vital improvement system by getting all employees involved. Train workers how to write improvement proposals, help supervisors promote participation, and put creative problem solving to work in your company. Designed as a self-trainer and study group tool, the book is heavily illustrated and includes hundreds of examples.
ISBN 0-915299-22-4 / 232 pages / $49.95 / Order code IDEA-BK

Productivity Press, Inc., Dept. BK, P.O. Box 3007, Cambridge, MA 02140 1-800-274-9911

The Improvement Book
Creating the Problem-Free Workplace
by Tomo Sugiyama

A practical guide to setting up a participatory problem- solving system in the workplace. This book provides clear direction for starting a problem-free engineering program, a full introduction to basic concepts of industrial housekeeping (known in Japan as 5S), two chapters of examples that can be used in small group training activities, and a workbook for individual use. Informal, using many anecdotes and examples, this book provides a proven fundamental approach to problem solving for any industrial setting.
ISBN 0-915299-47-X / 320 pages / $49.95 / Order code IB-BK

JIT Factory Revolution
Hiroyuki Hirano/JIT Management Library

Here at last is the first-ever encyclopedic picture book of JIT. Using 240 pages of photos, cartoons, and diagrams, this unprecedented behind-the-scenes look at actual production and assembly plants shows you exactly how JIT looks and functions. It shows you how to set up each area of a JIT plant and provides hundreds of useful ideas you can implement. If you've made the crucial decision to run production using JIT and want to show your employees what it's all about, this book is a must. The photographs, from various Japanese production and assembly plants, provide vivid depictions of what work is like in a JIT environment. And the text, simple and easy to read, makes all the essentials crystal clear.
ISBN 0-915299-44-5 / 240 pages / $49.95 / Order code JITFAC-BK

Today and Tomorrow
by Henry Ford

The inspiration for Just-In-Time. Originally published in 1926, this autobiography by the world's most famous automaker has been long out of print. Yet Ford's ideas have never stopped having an impact, and this book provides direct access to the thinking that changed industry forever. Here is the man who doubled wages, cut the price of a car in half, and produced over 2 million units a year. Time has not diminished the progressiveness of his business philosophy, or his profound influence on worldwide industry. You will be enlightened by what you read, and intrigued by the words of this colorful and remarkable man.
ISBN 0-915299-36-4 / 286 pages / $24.95 / Order code FORD-BK

Productivity Press, Inc., Dept. BK, P.O. Box 3007, Cambridge, MA 02140 1-800-274-9911

TO ORDER: Write, phone, or fax Productivity Press, Dept. BK, P.O. Box 3007, Cambridge, MA 02140, phone 1-800-274-9911, fax 617-868-3524. Send check or charge to your credit card (American Express, Visa, MasterCard accepted).

U.S. ORDERS: Add $4 shipping for first book, $2 each additional. CT residents add 7.5% and MA residents 5% sales tax.

FOREIGN ORDERS: Payment must be made in U.S. dollars, with checks drawn on U.S. banks. For Canadian orders, add $10 shipping for first book, $2 each additional. Orders to other countries are on a pro forma basis; please indicate shipping method desired.

NOTE: Prices are subject to change without notice.

BOOKS AVAILABLE FROM PRODUCTIVITY PRESS

Buehler, Vernon M. and Y.K. Shetty (eds.). **Competing Through Productivity and Quality**
ISBN 0-915299-43-7 / 1989 / 576 pages / $39.95 / order code COMP

Christopher, William F. **Productivity Measurement Handbook**
ISBN 0-915299-05-4 / 1985 / 680 pages / $137.95 / order code PMH

Ford, Henry. **Today and Tomorrow**
ISBN 0-915299-36-4 / 1988 / 286 pages / $24.95 / order code FORD

Fukuda, Ryuji. **Managerial Engineering: Techniques for Improving Quality and Productivity in the Workplace**
ISBN 0-915299-09-7 / 1984 / 206 pages / $34.95 / order code ME

Hatakeyama, Yoshio. **Manager Revolution! A Guide to Survival in Today's Changing Workplace**
ISBN 0-915299-10-0 / 1985 / 208 pages / $24.95 / order code MREV

Hirano, Hiroyuki. **JIT Factory Revolution: A Pictorial Guide to Factory Design of the Future**
ISBN 0-915299-44-5 / 1989 / 208 pages / $49.95 / order code JITFAC

Japan Human Relations Association (ed.). **The Idea Book: Improvement Through TEI (Total Employee Involvement)**
ISBN 0-915299-22-4 / 1988 / 232 pages / $49.95 / order code IDEA

Japan Management Association (ed.). **Kanban and Just-In-Time at Toyota: Management Begins at the Workplace** (Revised Ed.), *Translated by David J. Lu*
ISBN 0-915299-48-8 / 1989 / 192 pages / $34.95 / order code KAN

Japan Management Association and Constance E. Dyer. **The Canon Production System: Creative Involvement of the Total Workforce**
ISBN 0-915299-06-2 / 1987 / 251 pages / $36.95 / order code CAN

Karatsu, Hajime. **Tough Words For American Industry**
ISBN 0-915299-25-9 / 1988 / 178 pages / $24.95 / order code TOUGH

Karatsu, Hajime. **TQC Wisdom of Japan: Managing for Total Quality Control,** *Translated by David J. Lu*
ISBN 0-915299-18-6 / 1988 / 125 pages / $34.95 / order code WISD

Lu, David J. **Inside Corporate Japan: The Art of Fumble-Free Management**
ISBN 0-915299-16-X / 1987 / 278 pages / $24.95 / order code ICJ

Monden, Yashuhiro and Sakurai, Michiharu. **Japanese Management Accounting**
ISBN 0-915299-50-X / 1989 / 512 pages / $49.95 / order code JMACT

Mizuno, Shigeru (ed.). **Management for Quality Improvement: The 7 New QC Tools**
ISBN 0-915299-29-1 / 1988 / 304 pages / $59.95 / order code 7TQC

Nakajima, Seiichi. **Introduction to TPM: Total Productive Maintenance**
ISBN 0-915299-23-2 / 1988 / 129 pages / $39.95 / order code ITPM

Productivity Press, Inc., Dept. BK, P.O. Box 3007, Cambridge, MA 02140 1-800-274-9911

Nakajima, Seiichi. **TPM Development Program: Implementing Total Productive Maintenance**
ISBN 0-915299-37-2 / 1989 / 528 pages / $85.00 / order code DTPM

Nikkan Kogyo Shimbun, Ltd./Factory Magazine (ed.). **Poka-yoke: Improving Product Quality by Preventing Defects**
ISBN 0-915299-31-3 / 1989 / 288 pages / $59.95 / order code IPOKA

Ohno, Taiichi. **Toyota Production System: Beyond Large-Scale Production**
ISBN 0-915299-14-3 / 1988 / 162 pages / $39.95 / order code OTPS

Ohno, Taiichi. **Workplace Management**
ISBN 0-915299-19-4 / 1988 / 165 pages / $34.95 / order code WPM

Ohno, Taiichi and Setsuo Mito. **Just-In-Time for Today and Tomorrow: A Total Management System**
ISBN 0-915299-20-8 / 1988 / 208 pages / $34.95 / order code OMJIT

Psarouthakis, John. **Better Makes Us Best**
ISBN 0-915299-56-9 / 1989 / 112 pages / $16.95 / order code BMUB

Shingo, Shigeo. **Non-Stock Production: The Shingo System for Continuous Improvement**
ISBN 0-915299-30-5 / 1988 / 480 pages / $75.00 / order code NON

Shingo, Shigeo. **A Revolution In Manufacturing: The SMED System,** *Translated by Andrew P. Dillon*
ISBN 0-915299-03-8 / 1985 / 383 pages / $65.00 / order code SMED

Shingo, Shigeo. **The Sayings of Shigeo Shingo: Key Strategies for Plant Improvement,** *Translated by Andrew P. Dillon*
ISBN 0-915299-15-1 / 1987 / 207 pages / $36.95 / order code SAY

Shingo, Shigeo. **A Study of the Toyota Production System from an Industrial Engineering Viewpoint** (Revised Ed.)
ISBN 0-915299-17-8 / 1989 / 400 pages / $TBA / order code STREV

Shingo, Shigeo. **Zero Quality Control: Source Inspection and the Poka-yoke System,** *Translated by Andrew P. Dillon*
ISBN 0-915299-07-0 / 1986 / 328 pages / $65.00 / order code ZQC

Shinohara, Isao (ed.). **New Production System: JIT Crossing Industry Boundaries**
ISBN 0-915299-21-6 / 1988 / 224 pages / $34.95 / order code NPS

Sugiyama, Tomō. **The Improvement Book: Creating the Problem-free Workplace**
ISBN 0-915299-47-X / 1989 / 320 pages / $49.95 / order code IB-BK

Tateisi, Kazuma. **The Eternal Venture Spirit: An Executive's Practical Philosophy**
ISBN 0-915299-55-0 / 1989 / 208 pages / $19.95 / order code EVS

AUDIO-VISUAL PROGRAMS

Japan Management Association. **Total Productive Maintenance: Maximizing Productivity and Quality**
ISBN 0-915299-46-1 / 167 slides / 1989 / $749.00 / order code STPM
ISBN 0-915299-49-6 / 2 videos / 1989 / $749.00 / order code VTPM

Shingo, Shigeo. **The SMED System,** *Translated by Andrew P. Dillon*
ISBN 0-915299-11-9 / 181 slides / 1986 / $749.00 / order code S5
ISBN 0-915299-27-5 / 2 videos / 1987 / $749.00 / order code V5

Shingo, Shigeo. **The Poka-yoke System,** *Translated by Andrew P. Dillon*
ISBN 0-915299-13-5 / 235 slides / 1987 / $749.00 / order code S6
ISBN 0-915299-28-3 / 2 videos / 1987 / $749.00 / order code V6

TO ORDER: Write, phone, or fax Productivity Press, Dept. BK, P.O. Box 3007, Cambridge, MA 02140, phone 1-800-274-9911, fax 617-868-3524. Send check or charge to your credit card (American Express, Visa, MasterCard accepted).

U.S. ORDERS: Add $4 shipping for first book, $2 each additional. CT residents add 7.5% and MA residents 5% sales tax.

FOREIGN ORDERS: Payment must be made in U.S. dollars (checks must be drawn on U.S. banks). For Canadian orders, add $10 shipping for first book, $2 each additional. For orders to other countries write, phone, or fax for quote and indicate shipping method desired.

NOTE: Prices subject to change without notice.

UTAH STATE UNIVERSITY PARTNERS PROGRAM

Shigeo Shingo Prize for
Manufacturing Excellence

announces the

Shigeo Shingo Prizes for Manufacturing Excellence

*Awarded for Manufacturing
Excellence Based on the
Work of Shigeo Shingo*

*for North American Businesses,
Students and Faculty*

ELIGIBILITY

Businesses: Applications are due in late January. They should detail the quality and productivity improvements achieved through Shingo's manufacturing methods and similar techniques. Letters of intent are required by mid-November of the previous year.

Students: Applicants from accredited schools must apply by letter before November 15, indicating what research is planned. Papers must be received by early March.

Faculty: Applicants from accredited schools must apply by letter before November 15, indicating the scope of papers planned, and submit papers by the following March.

CRITERIA

Businesses: Quality and productivity improvements achieved by using Shingo's Scientific Thinking Mechanism (STM) and his methods, such as Single-Minute-Exchange of Die (SMED), Poka-yoke (defect prevention), Just-In-Time (JIT), and Non-Stock Production (NSP), or similar techniques.

Students: Creative research on quality and productivity improvements through the use and extension of Shingo's STM and his manufacturing methods: SMED, NSP, and Poka-yoke.

Faculty: Papers publishable in professional journals based on empirical, conceptual or theoretical applications and extensions of Shingo's manufacturing methods for quality and productivity improvements: SMED, Poka-yoke, JIT, and NSP.

PRIZES

Awards will be presented by Shigeo Shingo at Utah State University's annual Partners Productivity Seminar, held in April in Logan, Utah.

Five graduate and five undergraduate student awards of $2,000, $1,500, and $1,000 to first, second, and third place winners, respectively, and $500 to fourth and fifth place winners.

Three faculty awards of $3,000, $2,000 and $1,000, respectively.

Six Shigeo Shingo Medallions to the top three large and small business winners.

SHINGO PRIZE COMMITTEE

Committee members representing prestigious business, professional, academic and governmental organizations worldwide will evaluate the applications and select winners, assisted by a technical examining board.

Application forms and contest information may be obtained from the Shingo Prize Committee, College of Business, UMC 3521, Utah State University, Logan, UT, 84322, 801-750-2281. All English language books by Dr. Shingo can be purchased from the publisher, Productivity Press, P.O. Box 3007, Cambridge, MA 02140: call 1-800-274-9911 or 617-497-5146.

Japan's "Dean of Quality Consultants"

Dr. Shigeo Shingo is, quite simply, the world's leading expert on improving the manufacturing process. Known as "Dr. Improvement" in Japan, he is the originator of the Single-Minute Exchange of Die (SMED) concept and the Poka-yoke defect prevention system and one of the developers of the Just-In-Time production system that helped make Toyota the most productive automobile manufacturer in the world. His work now helps hundreds of other companies worldwide save billions of dollars in manufacturing costs annually.

The most sought-after consultant in Japan, Dr. Shingo has trained more than 10,000 people in 100 companies. He established and is President of Japan's highly-regarded Institute of Management Improvement and is the author of numerous books, including *Revolution in Manufacturing: The SMED System* and *Zero Quality Control: Source Inspection and the Poka-yoke System*. His newest book, *Non-Stock Production*, concentrates on expanding U.S. manufacturers' understanding of stockless production.

Dr. Shingo's genius is his understanding of exactly why products are manufactured the way they are, and then transforming that understanding into a workable system for low-cost, high-quality production. In the history of international manufacturing, Shingo stands alongside such pioneers as Robert Fulton, Henry Ford, Frederick Taylor, and Douglas McGregor as one of the key figures in the quest for improvement.

His world-famous SMED system is known as "The Heart of Just-In-Time Manufacturing" for (1) reducing set-up time from hours to minutes; (2) cutting lead time from months to days; (3) slashing work-in-progress inventory by up to 90%; (4) involving employees in team problem solving; (5) 99% improvement in quality; and (6) 70% reduction in floor space.

Shigeo Shingo has been called the father of the second great revolution in manufacturing.
— Quality Control Digest

The money-saving, profit-making ideas... set forth by Shingo could do much to help U.S. manufacturers reduce set-up time, improve quality and boost productivity ... all for very little cash.
Tooling & Production Magazine

When Americans think about quality today, they often think of Japan. But when the Japanese think of quality, they are likely to think of Shigeo Shingo,... architect of Toyota's now famous production system.
Boardroom Report

Shingo's visit to our plant was significant in making breakthroughs in productivity we previously thought impossible. The benefits... are more far-reaching than I ever anticipated.
Gifford M. Brown, Plant Mgr.
Ford Motor Company